DISCOVERING AMERICA

Territories and Possessions

**PUERTO RICO • U.S. VIRGIN ISLANDS • GUAM
AMERICAN SAMOA • WAKE, MIDWAY, AND OTHER ISLANDS
MICRONESIA**

By
Thomas G. Aylesworth
Virginia L. Aylesworth

CHELSEA HOUSE PUBLISHERS
New York • Philadelphia

3   5   7   9   8   6   4

Library of Congress Cataloging-in-Publication Data

Aylesworth, Thomas G.
    Territories and possessions: Puerto Rico, U.S. Virgin Islands, Guam,
American Samoa, Wake, Midway, and other islands, Micronesia
Thomas G. Aylesworth, Virginia L. Aylesworth.
        p. cm.—(Discovering America)
    Includes bibliographical references and index.
    ISBN 0-7910-3413-5.
        0-7910-3431-3 (pbk.)
    1. United States—Territories and possessions—Juvenile literature. [1. United States—Insular
possessions. 2. United States—Territories and possessions.] I. Aylesworth, Virginia L. II.
Title. III. Series: Aylesworth, Thomas G. Discovering America.

F970.A95   1996   94-45827
909'.0971273—dc20   CIP
                                             AC

CONTENTS

Puerto Rico

In the center of the seal of the Commonwealth of Puerto Rico is a lamb, symbolizing St. John, holding a white banner and rests on the Book of Revelation. The lamb also represents peace and brotherhood. The Commonwealth's motto forms a semicircle around the bottom of the seal. The letters "F" and "I" at the top stand for King Ferdinand and Queen Isabella of Spain. Symbols of the kingdom of Spain decorate the border surrounding the seal, which was given to settlers by King Ferdinand in 1511.

Capital: San Juan

Commonwealth Flag

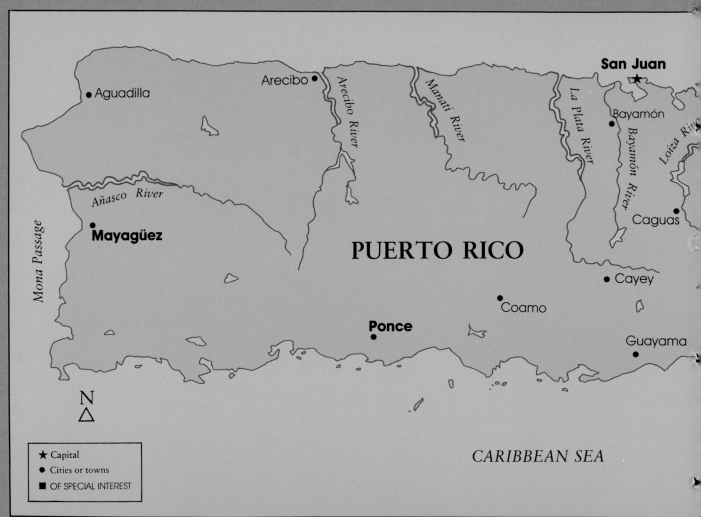

PUERTO RICO
At a Glance

Commonwealth Tree: Ceiba (Silk-cotton tree)

Commonwealth Song: "La Borinqueña"

Commonwealth Flower: Maga

Commonwealth Bird: Reinita

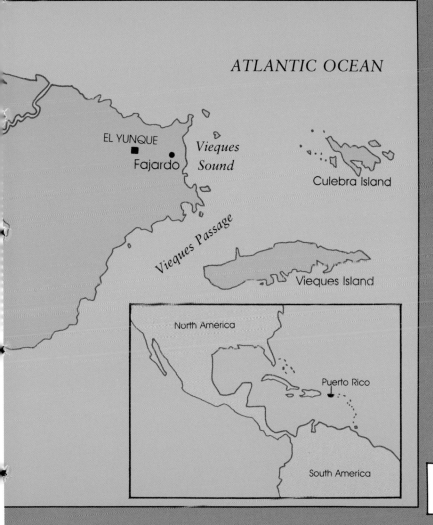

Major Crops: Sugar cane, tobacco, bananas, citrus fruits

Major Industries: Pharmaceuticals, chemicals, machinery

Size: 3,492 square miles
Population: 3,580,332

Commonwealth Flag

The flag of the Commonwealth of Puerto Rico was designed about 1895 and officially adopted in 1952. A five-pointed, white star in the center of a blue triangle appears to the left of the banner. The rest of the flag consists of five alternating horizontal red and white stripes.

Commonwealth Motto
Joannes Est Nomen Ejus

The Latin motto of Puerto Rico means, "John is his name." It is taken from the New Testament and refers to Saint John the Baptist.

The sun sets over Puerto Rico.

Commonwealth Capital

Caparra, founded in 1508 by Ponce de León, was the first capital of Puerto Rico. San Juan has been the island's capital since 1521. The present capitol building, designed by Rafael Carmoega and built of Georgia marble, resembles the Capitol in Washington, D.C.

Commonwealth Name and Nickname

Puerto Rico was originally called *Borinquen* by the native Arawak Indians. When Christopher Columbus discovered the island on November 19, 1493, he named it San Juan Bautista. The name Puerto Rico, which is Spanish for "rich harbor," originally applied to the capital city. Eventually, the name was used to refer to the entire island. Puerto Rico has also been called the *Island of Enchantment*.

Commonwealth Flower

The maga is the flower of the Commonwealth of Puerto Rico.

Commonwealth Tree

The ceiba, or silk-cotton tree, is the tree of the Commonwealth of Puerto Rico. The silky fiber kapok comes from this large tropical plant.

Commonwealth Bird

The reinita is the bird of the Commonwealth of Puerto Rico.

Commonwealth National Anthem

The national anthem of Puerto Rico is "La Borinqueña," with music by Felix Astol y Artés. Words were later added by Lola Rodríguez de Tío.

Population

The population of Puerto Rico in 1992 was estimated to

The Camuy Caves of Rio Camuy Cave Park belong to one of the largest subterranean cave networks in this hemisphere.

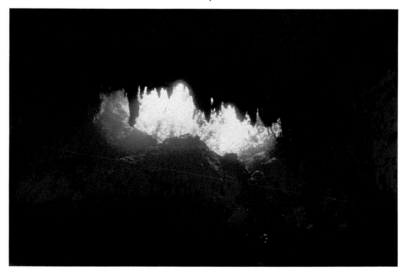

be 3,580,332. There are 1,030.9 people per square mile.

Industries

The principal industries of the island are agriculture and tourism. The chief manufactured products are pharmaceuticals, chemicals, metals, electric machinery and equipment, petroleum products, food products, and apparel.

Agriculture

The chief crops of the island are sugarcane, coffee, plantains, bananas, avocados, oranges, yams, taniers, pineapples, pidgeon peas, peppers, pumpkins, coriander, lettuce, and tobacco. Livestock is also important in Puerto Rico; there are estimated to be 600,000 cattle, 206,000 pigs, and 7.4 million chickens and turkeys on its farms. Cement, sand, and gravel are important mineral products. Commercial fishing earned $6.2 million in 1992.

Government

Puerto Rico is a commonwealth associated with the United States. The governor, who is elected to a four-year term, appoints other top officials. The legislature, which meets annually, consists of a 27-member senate and a 51-member house of representatives. Senators and representatives serve four-year terms. The most recent constitution was adopted in 1952. Puerto Ricans also elect a resident commissioner, who represents the common-wealth in the U.S. House of Representatives. The resident commissioner may vote in committee, but not on the floor of the House. The people of Puerto Rico are citizens of the United States, but do not vote in national elections. They do vote, however, in national primary elections.

Sports

Although cockfighting is a major sport in Puerto Rico,

A street corner in Old San Juan.

baseball might well be considered the national pastime. There are no professional teams on the major league level, but there is a Caribbean League with a season that runs from October through March. Stadiums are located in the

The trolley takes visitors on a tour of Old San Juan: the city was once enclosed by a wall and protected by fortresses.

cities of San Juan, Santurce, Ponce, Caguas, Arecibo, and Mayagüez. Basketball is also popular on the island. The Federación Nacional de Baloncesto de Puerto Rico has teams in most of the larger cities. Boxing and wrestling take place throughout the year. Popular participant sports include swimming, tennis, golf, and fishing.

Major Cities

San Juan (population 437,745). Settled in 1521 by Juan Ponce de León and about 50 Spanish colonists, Puerto Rico's capital is also the island's largest city. The city was subjected to frequent attacks by European privateers and fortifications were constructed to defend the city. San Juan, which had been the island's capital since 1521, maintained its status when Puerto Rico came under U.S. administration in 1898. The original city, "Old San Juan," is well preserved and serves as a major tourist attraction. It is an industrialized city and the center of manufacturing. Its products include: rum and other beverages, chemicals, clothing, drugs, jewelry, and cement. San Juan is the primary commercial, shipping, industrial, and governmental center of the Commonwealth of Puerto Rico and is a popular vacation resort with many beautiful beaches and luxury hotels.

Although the original San Juan Cathedral was destroyed by a hurricane, it was reconstructed in 1540 and stands today as a rare example of medieval architecture in the Americas.

Things to see in San Juan: Old San Juan, The Capitol, San Jeronimo Fort (1788), Ponce de León Museum, La Fortaleza, Casa Blanca (1523), Casa del Libro, Museum of the Seas, Capilla del Cristo, City Hall, Botanical Garden, Museum of Fine Arts, Plaza de San José, Casa del Callejón, Casa de los Contrafuertes, Dominican Convent, Plazuela de la Rogativa, Pablo Casals Museum, Plaza de Armas, La Intendencia, Plaza de Colón, San Juan Central Park, Muñoz Marín Park, El Arsenal, San José Church, Museo del Niño, San Juan Museum of Art and History, Pharmacy Museum, San Juan Cathedral, El Cañuelo, El Castillo de San Felipe del Morro, Fort San Cristóbal, San Juan Gate, and the City Walls.

Ponce (population 187,749). One of the oldest European settlements in the New World, it was founded in the early 16th century and named for the Spanish explorer Juan Ponce de León. Located on Puerto Rico's south coast, the island's second largest city, known as the "Pearl of the South," is the center of the island's sugar, rum, and textile industries. Its port, Playa de Ponce, handles much of the overseas trade of southern Puerto Rico and is

The Caribbean National Forest, the only tropical forest in the U.S. National Forest System, is usually referred to as El Yunque, named for the mountain in the area.

also a fishing and yachting center. Nearly 400 buildings throughout the city have been restored, and the wrought-iron balconies, gas lamps, Corinthian columns, and arches are reminiscent of its Spanish heritage.

> *Things to see in Ponce:* Alcaldía, Plaza del Mercado, El Vígia, Plaza Central, Cathedral of Our Lady of Guadalupe, Parque de Bombas, Toro Negro Forest, Hacienda Buena Vista (1833), Ponce Museum of Art, and Tibes Indian Ceremonial Center.

Places to Visit

The National Park Service maintains one area in Puerto Rico: San Juan National Historic Site.

Near Arecibo: Arecibo Observatory. This observatory is home to the world's largest radio/radar telescope, which is used to study deep-space objects, the planets, and Earth's atmosphere.

Bayamón: Francisco Oller Art and History Museum. This museum is home to a selection of the works of Puerto Rico's greatest artist.

Near Cataño: Barrilito Rum Distillery. A 200-year-old

plantation home and 150-year-old windmill stand on the grounds of this rum plant.

Near Fajardo: Caribbean National Forest. Commonly known as El Yunque, the only tropical U.S. national forest receives 240 inches of rain annually.

Near Hatillo: Río Camuy Cave Park. One of the largest underground river systems in the world runs through the large subterranean cave network of the park, which first opened to the public in 1987.

Loíza Aldea: Church of San Patricio. Constructed in 1645, the church is the oldest continually functioning church on Puerto Rico.

Mayagüez: Mayagüez Zoo. The zoo features more than 340 species of animals from around the world displayed in their natural settings.

La Parguera: Phosphorescent Bay. The waters of this bay shimmer and glow when disturbed, due to the countless microorganisms which live there.

San Germán: Cathedral de Porta Coeli. Built in 1606, the church has been restored as a museum, and houses many religious statues, paintings, mosaics, and

This statue of La Rogativa represents the Spanish Dominion and religion, and it stands near the governor's mansion in Old San Juan.

ornaments.

Near Utuado: Caguana Indian Ceremonial Park. This restored park was originally constructed by Taíno Indians more than 700 years ago for recreation and worship.

Events

There are many events and organizations that schedule activities of various kinds in the Commonwealth of Puerto Rico. Here are some of them.

Sports: Horse racing at El Comandante Racetrack (San Juan).

Arts and Crafts: Barranquitas Native Handicrafts Fair (Barranquitas), Jayuya Indian Festival (Jayuya), Summer Arts

Dancers romp through the streets; colorful festivals and musical events make Puerto Rico an exciting place to visit year round.

The Performing Arts Center in Santurce is an elegant building that presents some of the best concerts, plays, and musicals in the Caribbean.

Festival (San Juan), Vieques Cultural Festival (Vieques).

Music: Bomba y Plena Festival (Ponce), San Juan Symphony Orchestra (San Juan), San Juan City Ballet (San Juan), Pablo Casals Festival (San Juan), Annual Puerto Rican Music Festival (San Juan).

Entertainment: Flower Festival (Aibonito), Fiesta de Santiago Apostol (Loíza Aldea), Puerto Rican Food Show (Luquillo Beach), San Juan Carnival (San Juan), Tropical Flower Show (San Juan), Le Lo Lai (San Juan), San Juan Bautista Festival (San Juan), Puerto Rico Beauty Pageant (San Juan).

Tours: Bacardi Rum Distillery (Cataño).

Theater: Julia de Burgos Amphitheater (Río Piedras), Drama Festival (San Juan), Puerto Rican Theater Festival (San Juan), Tapia y Rivera Theater (San Juan), Institute of Puerto Rican Culture Theater (San Juan), Performing Arts Center (Santurce).

The many beaches and resorts like Guajataca, seen here, have made Puerto Rico a popular tourist attraction. The rugged coast on the north side of the island near Quebradillas is also celebrated for interesting limestone formations.

The Land and the Climate

The Commonwealth of Puerto Rico (or *Estado Libre Asociado de Puerto Rico*) is a large island between the Atlantic Ocean and the Caribbean Sea just west of the Dominican Republic. The easternmost of the West Indies island group called the Greater Antilles, it is 1,040 miles southeast of Miami, Florida. The commonwealth includes many smaller islands off the coast. Puerto Rico has four main land regions: the Coastal Lowlands, the Coastal Valleys, the Foothills, and the Central Mountains.

The Coastal Lowlands border the island's northern and southern coasts. The northern Coastal Lowlands extend from 8 to 12 miles inland, and their climate is humid. The southern Coastal Lowlands are narrower and drier. These lowlands are the site of Puerto Rico's largest cities, San Juan and Ponce, and most of the commonwealth's industries. Sugar cane is an important crop here.

The Coastal Valleys are found along the east and west coasts. Sugar cane farming is important here, too, and coconuts and fruits are cultivated.

The only one of the 155 National Forests that is tropical, El Yunque (The Anvil), 25 miles from San Juan, covers over 28,000 acres. The rain forest is dominated by two peaks, El Yunque, 3,493 feet, and El Toro, 3,526 feet, and is filled with 240 species of trees, countless birds and masses of flowers, including tuberoses, impatiens, and white ginger. El Yunque is also the home of the *coqui*, the tiny tree frog, whose night song resembles that of the nightingale.

Many farmers in the rugged hills still plow with a yoke of oxen. The main crops of the island are bananas, tobacco, sugar cane and citrus fruits.

The Foothills rise in both the north and the south, extending inland from the Coastal Lowlands. This hilly area has jagged peaks and round basins formed by water that eroded the limestone beneath the hills, causing the ground to sink.

The Central Mountains run east and west in the south-central part of the island. The main range here is called the Cordillera Central; another range, the Sierra de Luquillo, extends off to the northeast. In the Cordillera Central is the highest point in Puerto Rico—Cerro de Punta, 4,389 feet above sea level. The main crop in the western part of the mountains is coffee, and citrus fruits are also grown here. In the east, the most important crop is tobacco.

The coastline of the commonwealth measures some 311 miles. But if the coastlines of the small bays and inlets are included, the total is 700 miles. Along the coast are many beautiful sheltered beaches and harbors.

Local fruits, like mango, melons, grapefruit and papaya can be bought at market stands in the towns and cities across the island. Other street stands serve *pastelillos,* fried turnovers stuffed with meat or cheese; *chicharron,* pork cracklings; or *bacalito,* fried cod batter.

The nearby island of Vieques, a short ferry ride from Fajardo, on the east coast of Puerto Rico, offers secluded beaches of dazzling white sand.

The Arecibo is Puerto Rico's longest river, but none of the island's rivers is navigable by large boats. Their importance is as a source of water for hydroelectric power, industry, and irrigation.

The average all-year-round temperature is a delightful 76 degrees Fahrenheit in the coastal sections, although it is cooler in the mountains. There is only about a 6-degree F. difference between winter and summer. It is moderately humid during the summer months, but not uncomfortably so. Puerto Rico can claim almost perpetual sunshine: it has only about five cloudy days per year. Rainfall varies with location from about 40 to 150 inches annually, with 200 inches falling in the Caribbean National Forest at El Yunque Mountain. There are brief rain showers throughout the year, slightly more frequent between May and December.

Since Ponce de León cried, "¡Qué puerto rico!" (What a rich port) this beautiful Caribbean Island has captured the imagination of legions of people. With its warm climate, perpetually sunny beaches, and colorful culture, it is obvious why Puerto Rico has been called the *Island of Enchantment*.

The History

The Spanish explorer Juan Ponce de León established the first settlement on the island in 1508 and served as the governor. A local Taino Indian legend sent him in search of the fabled Fountain of Youth, and he discovered the Florida peninsula. His tomb is now in the Cathedral of San Juan.

Christopher Columbus discovered Puerto Rico on November 19, 1493, during his second voyage to the New World. He called it San Juan Bautista in honor of St. John the Baptist, as reflected in the commonwealth motto from the New Testament, "John Is His Name." Columbus landed on the northwest coast at a spot that is now Aguadilla. He claimed the island for Spain, but made no attempt at colonization.

The first colonizers were Spanish explorers led by Juan Ponce de León, who founded Caparra near San Juan Harbor, in 1508. Located between the present Santurce and Bayamón Districts, it was the second city in the New World. Later, for reasons of defense, the settlement was moved to present-day "Old San Juan" on an island in the bay. Upon arriving, Ponce de León reportedly exclaimed, "¡Qué puerto rico! (What a rich port!)," thus naming the area around the harbor. During the course of the island's history, the names of the capital and the island were transposed: Puerto Rico came to be used as the name of the island and San Juan as that of its capital. In 1514 the island was divided into two districts, each with its own administrator. The eastern section was referred to as Puerto Rico and the western section as San Germán.

After the Spanish settlement was established, the island's Arawak Indians tried to drive out the colonists, but they were attacked ruthlessly. Those who were not enslaved by the Spanish were killed, or succumbed to European diseases to which they had no immunity. By the mid-1500s, few Indians remained on the island that they had called Boriquen.

The settlers from Spain faced many difficulties, including frequent hurricanes, outbreaks of disease, and attacks by the Carib Indians, who lived on neighboring islands. British, French, and Dutch raiders plundered the island, and pirates were a constant threat. But the

The arcaded galleries of the courtyard of the Dominican Convent in San Juan are a fine example of Spanish colonial architecture. Built by the Dominican Friars in the 16th century, the convent has been restored and is used as a library and concert hall. Another wing houses the Pablo Casals Museum.

Depicted in an engraving dated 1860, the residents of San Juan stroll along the battlements of Fort San Cristobal. The forts of Puerto Rico were built to guard the treasure fleets from Spanish America.

Spanish population continued to grow, and forts and towns were built. Sugar cane was introduced in 1515, and slaves were imported from Africa three years later to work on the plantations.

Puerto Ricans began to demand greater independence from Spain during the 1850s, long after the great Spanish Empire of the 1500s was only a memory. In 1897 Spain did grant more local autonomy, and a new Puerto Rican government was set up shortly before the Spanish-American War broke out in 1898. U.S. troops landed on the south coast at Guánica, and Spanish troops retreated before them. The U.S. Navy bombarded San Juan, and the Puerto Ricans refused to cooperate with the Spanish army and navy; instead, they welcomed the American troops. On October 18, 1898, the island was surrendered, and Spain ceded Puerto Rico to the United States in the Treaty of Paris on December 10, 1898. The island remained under a U.S. military government for the next year and a half.

The American occupation meant that the use of U.S. money and postage on the island was official. In April 1900, Congress passed the Foraker Act, which instituted civil government. The arrangement did not please the Puerto Ricans, despite U.S. construction of dams, hospitals, roads, and schools. The Puerto Rican economy depended upon agriculture, and the people resented the fact that U.S. companies were skimming off much of the profit they made from their interests in local plantations and sugar mills.

The Jones Act of 1917 effected a great improvement. It made Puerto Rico a territory of the United States and granted U.S. citizenship to all who wanted it: only 288 people chose not to accept citizenship. Many Puerto Rican men served in the armed forces during World War I, still more during World War II.

Old San Juan, the oldest part of the city, has been lovingly restored and preserved, mixing small businesses with museums, and markets with old houses.

The most familiar landmark in Puerto Rico is El Morro, the great fortress built by the Spanish between 1540 and 1586. It has never been taken from the sea, although the English besieged it successfully in 1598. The Spanish won it back and improved the fortifications. Completed in 1783, it still guards the harbor of San Juan. The tracks for moving cannon to cover the widest field of fire created a pattern of arcs along the walls as seen above.

Rum, made from local sugar cane, distilled and bottled on the island, is one of the most popular local drinks. Puerto Rican rum is also exported all over the world.

One of the most impressive chapters in Puerto Rican history began in the early 1940s. It was "Operation Bootstrap," aimed at economic development that would make the island self-sufficient and raise its standard of living. Puerto Ricans and the U.S. government joined forces for the project. Large farms were broken up, and land was redistributed among farmers. Many old slum buildings were torn down and new housing went up. The educational system was overhauled.

The program was highly successful. New businesses produced chemical and pharmaceutical products, machinery, apparel, and other goods. By 1956 manufacturing had surpassed agriculture as the island's principal source of income, and it has remained in the lead ever since. Tourism has also become a major industry.

It was not until 1946 that Puerto Rico had its first native-born governor. He was Jesús Toribio Piñero, who was appointed by President Harry S. Truman. One year later, the island was given the right to elect its own governor; the first was Luis Muñoz Marín, who took office in 1948.

The Ponce Museum, designed by Edward Durrell Stone, houses a remarkable collection of Old Masters, including works by Rubens, Velázquez and Van Dyck. The Museum also contains many paintings by island and other Latin American artists.

On July 3, 1950, Puerto Rico was granted the right to draw up its own constitution, which was modeled on that of the United States. On July 25, 1952, Puerto Rico became a self-governing commonwealth. During the Korean War, the U.S. Army's 65th Infantry Regiment, made up of Puerto Ricans, won fame for its courage in battle.

Today Puerto Rico is still in a period of rapid industrial growth. Despite the increase in industry, the unemployment rate remains high, partly because of the island's high population density—987 people per square mile. Many Puerto Ricans have emigrated to the mainland in search of new opportunities. Puerto Ricans value their

The streets of San Juan are overhung with balconies, shading the doorways of the shops selling souvenirs, including *santos*, wooden carvings of the saints, as well as ceramics, baskets and *papier mache.*

Hispanic heritage, and the commonwealth offers many cultural facilities, including San Juan's Fine Arts Center and Puerto Rican Family Museum.

When Puerto Rico became a territory of the United States in 1898, only about 20 percent of its people could read or write. With the help of the federal government, public schools were established all over the island and the literacy rate improved dramatically. The University of Puerto Rico, founded in 1903, has its main campus at Rio Piedras and maintains a botanical garden and a Museum of Anthropology, Art, and History.

Arecibo Ionospheric Observatory, on the north side of the island, monitors changes in the layers of the earth's atmosphere.

The three-day fiesta of Santiago Apostal (St. James the Apostle), held in Loisa Aldea every July, combines the island's Spanish Catholic heritage with that of the African slaves who settled the town.

The People

More than 66 percent of Puerto Rico's people live in towns and cities, including San Juan, Ponce, and Mayaguez. More than 99 percent of them are of Hispanic descent, with a small number of Portuguese, Italians, French, and North Americans represented in the population. Some 80 percent of the people are Roman Catholics. Other denominations include the Assemblies of God, Baptists, Methodists, and Presbyterians.

Famous People

Many famous people were born in Puerto Rico. Here are a few:

Luis Arroyo b. 1927, Penuelas. Baseball pitcher

Herman Badillo b. 1929, Caguas. First U.S. congressman born in Puerto Rico

Carlos Romero Barcelo b. 1952, San Juan. Governor of Puerto Rico

Ramón Emeterio Betances 1827-98, near Cabo Rojo. Physician, writer, and political activist

Julia de Burgos 1914-53, Carolina. Poet

Orlando Cepeda b. 1937, Ponce. Baseball player

Roberto Clemente 1934-72, Carolina. Hall of Fame baseball player

Rafael Hernández Colón b. 1936, Ponce. Governor of Puerto Rico

Angel Cordero b. 1942, San Juan. Jockey

José Cruz b. 1947, Arroyo. Baseball player

Justino Díaz b. 1940, San Juan. Opera singer

Pablo Elvira b. 1938, Santurce. Opera singer

Sixto Escobar 1913-79, Barceloneta. Bantamweight boxing champion

José Feliciano b. 1945, Lares. Grammy Award-winning pop singer: *Light My Fire*

Luis A. Ferré b. 1904, Ponce. Governor of Puerto Rico

José Ferrer 1912-92, Santurce. Two-time Tony Award–winning stage actor and Academy Award–winning film actor: *Cyrano de Bergerac, The Shrike*

Ed Figueroa b. 1948, Ciales. Baseball pitcher

Felisa Rincón de Gautier b. 1897, Ceiba. Mayor of San Juan

Juan Gonzalez b. 1969, Vega Baja. Baseball player.

Guillermo Hernandez b. 1954, Aguada. Baseball pitcher

Raúl Julía 1940-94, San Juan. Stage and film actor: *Kiss of*

Roberto Clemente, the popular outfielder for the Pittsburgh Pirates, who won the National League batting championship four times, also directed Puerto Rican efforts to aid earthquake victims in Nicaragua. Clemente was killed in the crash of a plane carrying supplies to Nicaragua.

the Spider Woman, The Addams Family

Luis Muñoz Marín 1898-

1980, San Juan. First
elected governor of Puerto
Rico

Felix Millan b. 1943,
Yabucoa. Baseball player

Rita Moreno b. 1931,
Humacao. Academy
Award-winning film
actress and Tony Award-
winning stage actress: *West
Side Story, The Ritz*

Francisco Oller 1833-1917,
Bayamón. Artist

Jesús Toribio Piñero 1897-
1952, Carolina. First
native-born governor of
Puerto Rico

Miguel Piñero 1946-88,
Gurabo. Dramatist and
actor: *Short Eyes*

Juan Pizarro b. 1937,
Santurce. Baseball pitcher

Chi Chi Rodríguez b. 1934,
Río Piedras. Champion
golfer

Lola Rodríguez de Tío 1843-
1924, San Germán. Poet

Antonio Valero 1770-1863,
Fajardo. Military officer

Colleges and Universities

There are many colleges and
universities in Puerto Rico.
Here are the more prominent,
with their locations, dates of
founding, and undergraduate
enrollments.

Bayamón Central University,
Bayamón, 1961, 2,726

Caribbean University,
Bayamón, 1969, 13,041

*International American
University of Puerto Rico,
College of Arecibo*, Arecibo,
1957, 4,253; *Barranquitas
Regional College*,
Barranquitas, 1957, 1,484;
San Germán Campus, San
Germán, 1912, 5,239

Pontifical Catholic University of

Puerto Rico at Ponce, 1948,
11,055

Turabo University, Gurabo,
1972, 14,800

*Universidad Politecnica de
Puerto Rico*, Hato Rey, 1974,
4,322

*University of Puerto Rico Cayey
University College*, Cayey,
1967, 3,243; *Humacao
University College*,
Humacao, 1962, 3,896;
Mayagüez Campus,
Mayagüez, 1911, 9,885; *Río
Piedras*, Río Piedras, 1903,
16,729

University of the Sacred Heart,
Santurce, 1935, 5,404

Where To Get More Information

Puerto Rico Tourism Company
575 Fifth Avenue
New York, NY 10017
1-212-599-6262 or
1-800-223-6530

U.S. Virgin Islands

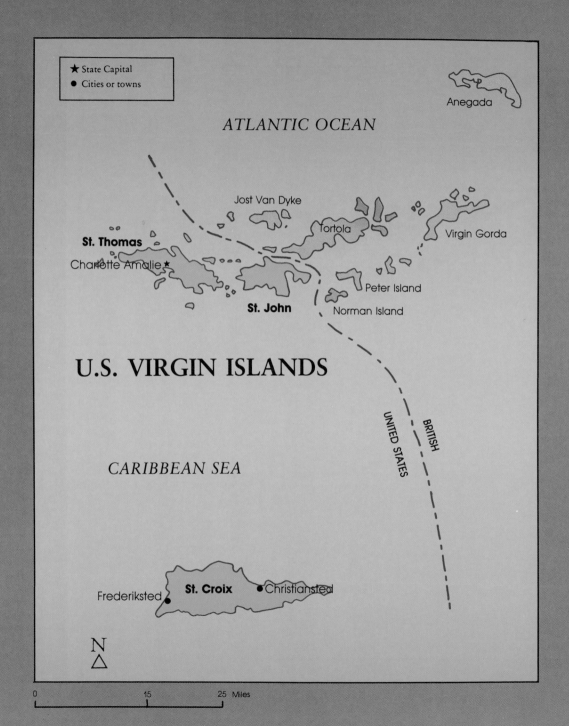

★ State Capital
● Cities or towns

ATLANTIC OCEAN

Anegada

Jost Van Dyke

Tortola

Virgin Gorda

St. Thomas

Charlotte Amalie ★

Peter Island

St. John

Norman Island

U.S. VIRGIN ISLANDS

UNITED STATES BRITISH

CARIBBEAN SEA

Frederiksted ● **St. Croix** ● Christiansted

N
△

0   15   25 Miles

THE U.S. VIRGIN ISLANDS
At a Glance

Flag

Major Industries: Tourism, rum, textiles, pharmaceuticals
Major Crops: Vegetables, sugar cane, nuts

Flower: Yellow Elder or Yellow Cedar
Bird: Yellow Breast
Song: "Virgin Islands March"

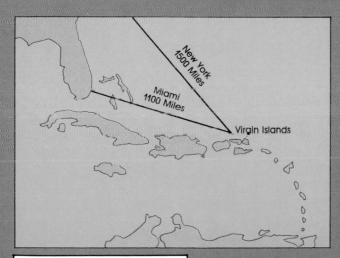

Size: 151 square miles
Population: 101,809

Capital: Charlotte Amalie, St. Thomas

Territorial Flag

The territorial flag of the U.S. Virgin Islands contains a golden American eagle centered on a white background. The eagle holds the shield of the United States on its breast, a green laurel branch in its right talon, and three arrows in its left talon. The letters "V" and "I" appear on either side of the eagle. The flag was adopted in 1917.

The tranquil blue waters of Cinnamon Bay on the island of St. John beckon bathers from all over the world.

Territorial Capital

Charlotte Amalie, on the island of St. Thomas, was chosen as territorial capital in 1917, when the United States purchased the islands from Denmark.

Territorial Name

Christopher Columbus named the islands *Las Virgenes* after St. Ursula and her followers. St. Ursula was the patron saint of British sailors.

Territorial Flower

The territorial flower of the U.S. Virgin Islands is the yellow elder, or yellow cedar, *Tecoma stans*, known by the local name Ginger Thomas. It was adopted by proclamation of Governor Paul Pearson in 1934.

Territorial Bird

The yellow breast, also called the sugar bird, is the territorial bird of the U.S. Virgin Islands.

Territorial Song

The territorial song of the

The U.S. Virgin Islands consist of over 50 islands. Some are large, dotted with volcanic hills, reefs, and lagoons, and some are just rocks jutting out from the sea.

U.S. Virgin Islands is "Virgin Islands March," with music by Alton A. Adams.

Population

The population of the U.S. Virgin Islands in 1992 was estimated to be 101,809. There are 748.6 persons per square mile.

Industries

The principal industries of the islands are tourism, aluminum ore refining, watch textiles, electronics, and petroleum refining. Tourism earned $662.8 million in 1988. The chief manufactured products are rum, textiles, concrete, watch making, pharmaceuticals, scientific instruments, food products, aluminum products, and perfumes.

Agriculture

The chief crops of the islands are sugarcane, nuts, tomatoes, lettuce, mangoes, bananas, cucumbers, and spinach. Livestock is also important to the U.S. Virgin Islands; there are estimated to be 3,762 cattle, 2,889 sheep, 4,035 goats, and 18,345 chickens on its farms. Sand and gravel are important mineral resources.

Government

The U.S. Virgin Islands is an organized unincorporated territory. The governor and lieutenant governor are elected to four-year terms. The unicameral, or one-house, legislature consists of 15 members elected to two-year terms. The legislature begins its session in January and meets again several times during the year. The Revised Organic Act of 1954 serves as the territory's constitution. Virgin Islanders also elect a delegate to the U.S. House of Representatives for a two-year term. This delegate may vote in committee but not on the floor of the House. Although

The Charlotte Amalie Harbor is the gateway to the island of St. Thomas and the most popular cruise port in the Caribbean.

Virgin Islanders are citizens of the United States, they do not vote in national elections.

Sports

Water sports dominate in the U.S. Virgin Islands. Sailing is extremely popular, as are surfing, deep-sea fishing, and diving.

Major Cities
Charlotte Amalie, St.

Thomas (population 12,331). By the mid-1700s, Charlotte Amalie had been declared a free port. Because of this, it became the home base of traders and pirates such as Blackbeard and Captain Kidd. While under Danish rule, the town was a center of one of the largest slave trade operations in the world. The territorial capital of the U.S. Virgin Islands, Charlotte Amalie is the only

town on the island of St. Thomas. The majority of people work for the government or in tourist-related industries.

Things to see in Charlotte Amalie: Blackbeard's Castle (1689), Bluebeard Castle, Government House (1867), Crown House (1750), St. Thomas Synagogue, the Dutch Reformed Church, Emancipation Park, Frederick Lutheran Church, Frenchtown, Grand Hotel (1841), Central Post Office, Hotel 1829 (1829), Legislative Building (1874), 99 Steps, Pissaro House, Fort Christian (1680), Market Square, New Herrnhut, and Royal Dane Mall.

Christiansted, St. Croix (population 2,555). The principal city of St. Croix, Christiansted briefly served as the capital of the Danish West Indies. The influence of the original Danish settlers can be seen in the city's numerous 18th-century buildings.

Things to see in Christiansted: Alexander Hamilton House (1750), Danish West India and

Christiansted is a beautiful harbor on the island of St. Croix, where a natural reef lies offshore, offering a haven for yachts and smaller boats.

Guinea Company Warehouse (1749), Fort Christiansvaern (1749), Government House (1747), Steeple Building, Old Danish Customs House (1734), and Scalehouse (1835).

Frederiksted, St. Croix (population 1,064). The emancipation of slaves on the islands was proclaimed at Fort Frederik on July 3, 1848. Thirty years later, much of the city was destroyed in a fire. Since then, it has been restored in Victorian style.

Things to see in Frederiksted: Apothecary Hall, Bellhouse, Customs House, Cruzan Rum Distillery, Judith's Fancy, Fort Frederik (1760), St Patrick's Roman Catholic Church (1843), St. Paul's Episcopal Church (1812), Victoria House (1803), and the Old Danish School.

Places to Visit

The National Park Service maintains three areas in the U.S. Virgin Islands: Buck Island Reef National Monument and Christiansted National Historic Site on St. Croix, and Virgin Islands National Park on St. John.

Fort Christian in St. Thomas is one of the oldest standing structures in the Virgin Islands. Dating back to 1672, it once housed the entire St. Thomas colony.

The Annaberg Ruins on St. John are the remains of an 18th-century sugar plantation and mill.

Coki Point: Coral World. Visitors descend to the ocean floor in this underwater observatory, where they may see fish, coral formations, and deep-water flowers.

Near Frederiksted: St. George Village Botanical Garden. This 17-acre tropical garden contains ruins of a 19th-century rum factory and workers' village.
Whim Greathouse. Restored buildings include the main house, windmill, watch house and bathhouse, cookhouse and apothecary, museum, and gift shop.

Near Leinster Bay: Annaberg Plantation. The plantation includes the ruins of an 18th-century sugar estate and mill, which have been partially restored.

Near Magens Bay: Drake's Seat. Sir Francis Drake is said to have observed his fleet and watched for enemy ships from this point, which offers a panoramic view of the St. Thomas region.

Sugar Loaf Hill: Christ of the Caribbean. This statue, overlooking Hawksnest, Trunk, and Cinnamon bays, was built in 1953 by Colonel Julius Wadsworth with Terrance Powell.

Events

Sports: Horse racing at Flamboyant Park (St. Croix), Coral Bay Regatta (St. John), "Around St. John Race" (St. John), horse racing at Nadir Race Track (St. Thomas), Virgin Islands Open Blue Marlin Fishing Tournament (St. Thomas), Hook In & Hold On Boardsailing Regatta (St. Thomas), Little Switzerland Tennis Tournament (St. Thomas), International Rolex Cup Regatta (St. Thomas).

Arts and Crafts: Arts Festival (St. Croix), "Arts Alive!" (St. Thomas).

Music: Caribbean Dance Company (St. Croix), Festival of the Arts (St. John), J'Ouvert Morning Tramp (St. Thomas).

Entertainment: Crucian Christmas Festival (St. Croix), Carnival (St. John), Carnival (St. Thomas), Market Square Food Festival (St. Thomas), Virgin Islands Charter Yacht Show (St. Thomas).

Tours: *Atlantis* Submarines (Charlotte Amalie), House Tours (St. Croix), Cruzan Rum Pavilion (St. Croix).

Theater: Island Center (St. Croix), Dorsch Cultural Center (St. Croix), Reichhold Center of the Performing Arts (St. Thomas).

Judah P. Benjamin was one of the earliest Southern senators to advocate secession during the Civil War.

The Land and the Climate

The U.S. Virgin Islands are about 40 miles east of Puerto Rico, along the Anegada Passage between the Atlantic Ocean and the Caribbean Sea. They include the islands of St. Croix, St. John, and St. Thomas, and many nearby islets. Together with the nearby British Virgin Islands, the group forms the westernmost part of a great chain of West Indian islands called the Lesser Antilles.

The U.S. Virgin Islands are volcanic in origin, and, except for St. Croix, they have rugged, hilly surfaces. Hills on the three major islands can reach heights of 1,500 feet above sea level. Tropical flowers and trees flourish, contributing to the islands' scenic beauty.

St. Croix, the largest of the Virgin Islands, covers 84 square miles and has almost half the islands' total population. St. John has an area of about 20 square miles, three-quarters of which comprises part of the Virgin Islands National Park. St. Thomas covers 28 square miles, and contains the highest point on the islands—Crown Mountain—at 1,556 feet. The remaining islands are too small to be inhabited.

With temperature ranges between 70 and 90 degrees Fahrenheit all year round, the U.S. Virgin Islands have a congenial climate. Trade winds moderate heat and humidity and rainfall averages 45 inches yearly, with the heaviest rains occurring in spring and fall. However, the islands frequently experience a water shortage because of increases in both population and tourism. By law, each house must have its own cistern to catch rain water, the size of the cistern based upon the area of the roof. There are seawater distillation plants on St. Thomas and St. Croix, but fresh water has to be imported from Puerto Rico during droughts.

Magen's Bay, on the Atlantic side of the island of St. Thomas, has clear water surrounded by over a mile of white sand, and remarkable tropical plants among the palm groves. It is considered one of the most beautiful beaches in the world.

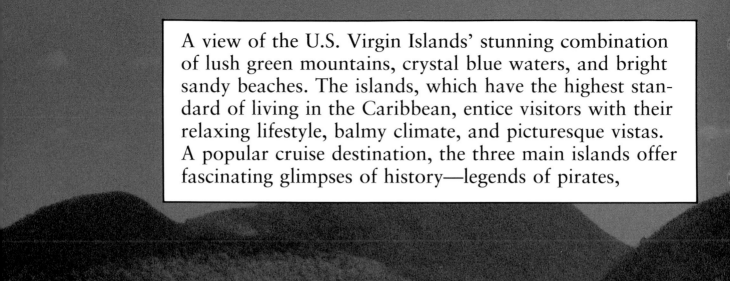

A view of the U.S. Virgin Islands' stunning combination of lush green mountains, crystal blue waters, and bright sandy beaches. The islands, which have the highest standard of living in the Caribbean, entice visitors with their relaxing lifestyle, balmy climate, and picturesque vistas. A popular cruise destination, the three main islands offer fascinating glimpses of history—legends of pirates,

quaint Danish architecture, and remains of sugar plantations—as well as tropical beauty. The waters surrounding the Virgin Islands also contain some of the most gorgeous coral reefs and tropical fish in the Caribbean.

Christopher Columbus, a Genovese sailor, is traditionally credited with the discovery of the New World. He did have the idea to sail west to reach to Spice Islands, and convinced King Ferdinand and Queen Isabella of Spain to sponsor a voyage. His small fleet of three ships left Spain on August 3, 1492, and made a landfall at San Salvador, which Columbus believed to be part of Japan, on October 12. He made three subsequent voyages and discovered Puerto Rico, Jamaica and Trinidad. A contemporary wrote that "as a seaman, he had no equal in his generation." The voyages of Columbus drew the American continents into the mainstream of history, while the riches of the new lands gave impetus to the rise of capitalism by adding to the depleted stock of European precious metals, and the balance of political and economic power shifted from the Mediterranean to the Atlantic coast.

The History

Christopher Columbus named the Virgin Islands and claimed them for Spain on his second voyage to the New World, in 1493. The islands were inhabited by the cannibalistic Carib Indians, who had a small battle with Columbus's crew at Sugar Bay, on St. Croix. The Indians repelled all visitors to their islands until the mid-1500s, when Emperor Charles V of Spain ordered his soldiers to kill them and seize their lands. Those who were not annihilated left the islands before they were taken over by the British and the Danes, who began settling there in the 1600s.

The British came to the Virgin Islands in 1607 on their way to set up the colony of Jamestown, Virginia. At the time, the Spaniards were using the islands' harbors to hide their treasure ships from pirates, but they never settled there. The first European settlers arrived in 1625, when Dutch and British colonists landed on St. Croix. They were driven out in the mid-1600s by Spaniards from Puerto Rico. Twenty years later, the French expelled the Spanish. The French controlled St. Croix until 1733, when they sold it to Denmark for $150,000.

The sugar mill under restoration at Whim Great House, one of the rich sugar plantations built on St. Croix during the 1790s. The sugar economy collapsed in the 19th century following a drop in sugar prices, restrictive import taxes and the emancipation of the slaves in 1848.

The walls of the buildings along Alexander Hamilton Alley in Christiansted were built three feet thick to keep the interior rooms cool. Hamilton, though born on the nearby island of Nevis, grew up on St. Croix, and worked as a clerk in a counting house in Christiansted.

The Danes had claimed St. Thomas by founding a settlement there in 1666, but the colony failed. A successful settlement was made in 1672, and the Danes finally settled on St. John in 1717, when the St. Thomas colony was well established. The Danish West India Company controlled the region's development for a hundred years. Slaves were imported to work on sugar-cane and cotton plantations, and St. Thomas was designated a duty-free port to enhance its commercial importance. Slave uprisings beginning in 1733, the year that Denmark purchased St. Croix, finally resulted in the abolition of slavery in 1848.

The Danish West Indies surrendered to the British twice during the Napoleonic Wars of the early 19th century. During these periods of occupation, so many English-speaking soldiers and sailors were quartered on the islands that English became the common language of the people.

From 1672 onward, the British controlled the rest of the Virgin Islands, separated from the Danish holdings by a channel called the Narrows. These 32 small islands, of which the largest are Anegada, Jost van Dyke, Tortola, and Virgin Gorda, are still a territory of Great Britain.

Denmark's attempts to develop the Virgin Islands during the latter part of the 19th century were largely unsuccessful, and in 1917 they were sold to the United States for $25,000,000. This purchase provided the United States with a base from which to safeguard the Panama Canal, which had been completed in 1914.

The people of the U.S. Virgin Islands were made citizens of the United States in 1927. After World War II, the federal government set aside some $10,000,000 to improve the islands' schools, hospitals, roads, and sewage and water systems. A new legislature was created in 1955, and three years later the islands' first native-born governor, John D. Merwin, was elected. After 1945, a shortage of workers led companies to offer higher wages to attract foreign workers to the islands. This resulted in tensions between immigrants and natives, who continued to receive lower wages. Natives of the Virgin Islands were also upset that nonnative white citizens controlled the economy.

Between 1960 and 1990 the population of the Virgin Islands tripled as many people left other Caribbean Islands in search of better living conditions and job opportunities. In 1962 the College of the Virgin Islands was established, and there are now campuses on St. Thomas and St. Croix. The Virgin Islands enjoy the highest standard of living of all the islands in the Caribbean.

The People

About 15 percent of the people in the U.S. Virgin Islands live in the cities of Charlotte Amalie, Christiansted, and Frederiksted. Some 63 percent were born in the islands and 12 percent in Puerto Rico. Other residents come from various parts of the West Indies and North America. The largest religious groups are the Episcopalians, Lutherans, Methodists, Moravians, and Roman Catholics.

Famous People

Many famous people were born in the U.S. Virgin Islands. Here are a few:

Sosthenes Behn 1882-1957, St. Thomas. Telephone corporation executive

Judah P. Benjamin 1811-64, St. Croix. Scholar, lawyer, and politician

Hugo Owen Bornn 1902-66, St. Thomas. Musician, composer, and educator

Almeris L. Christian b. 1919, St. Croix. U.S. federal court judge

Joe Christopher b. 1935, Frederiksted. Baseball player

Horace Clarke b. 1940, Frederiksted. Baseball player

Frank R. Crosswaith 1892-1965, St. Croix. Labor organizer

Jacob M. Da Costa 1833-1900, St. Thomas. Physician and educator

Melvin Evans b. 1917,

Camille Pissaro left the Virgin Islands at the age of 25 to become an impressionist painter in Paris. He was the only artist to exhibit in all eight impressionist shows.

Christiansted. First popularly elected governor of the U.S. Virgin Islands

Kelsey Grammer b. 1950?, St. Thomas. Emmy Award–winning television actor: *Frasier; Cheers*

Emile Griffith b. 1938, St. Thomas. Welterweight and middleweight boxing champion

Ellie Hendricks b. 1940, Charlotte Amalie. Baseball player

Roy Innis b. 1934, St. Croix. Civil rights leader

David H. Jackson 1884-1946, St. Croix. Lawyer, politician, and labor organizer

Al McBean b. 1938, Charlotte Amalie. Baseball pitcher

Jose Morales b. 1944, Frederiksted. Baseball player

Camille Pissaro 1830-1903, St. Thomas. Artist

Terence Todman b. 1926, St. Thomas. U.S. ambassador

Where To Get More Information

U.S. Virgin Islands Division of Tourism
1270 Avenue of the Americas
New York, NY 10020
1-212-582-4520

Guam

Windsurfing in Tumon Bay is a popular pastime for people who enjoy the outdoors.

GUAM

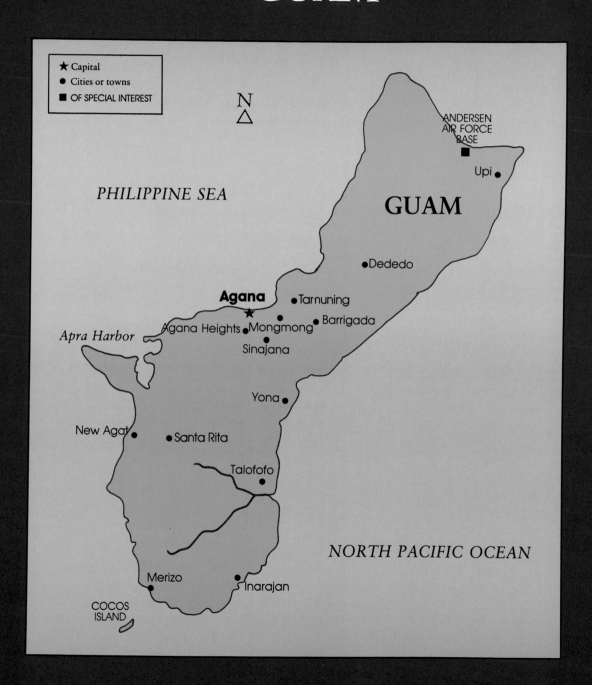

Legend:
- ★ Capital
- ● Cities or towns
- ■ OF SPECIAL INTEREST

N △

PHILIPPINE SEA

GUAM

ANDERSEN AIR FORCE BASE

Upi ●

● Dededo

Agana ★

● Tarnuning

Agana Heights ● ● Mongmong ● Barrigada

Apra Harbor

● Sinajana

Yona ●

New Agat ●

● Santa Rita

Talofofo ●

NORTH PACIFIC OCEAN

Merizo ●

● Inarajan

COCOS ISLAND

GUAM
At a Glance

Flag

Capital: Agana

Flower: Puti Tai Nobio (Bougainvillea)

Bird: Toto (Fruit Dove)

Tree: Ifit (Intsiabijuga)

Nickname: Where America's Day Begins

Song: "Stand Ye Guamanians"

Major Industries: Tourism, textiles, foods, petroleum refining

Major Crops: Cabbages, cucumbers, tomatoes, coconuts, yams

Size: 217 square miles
Population: 133,152

Territorial Flag

The territorial flag of Guam, adopted in 1917, contains the great seal centered on a blue field. The flag is edged with a narrow red border and a wider white border.

Territorial Motto

Where America's Day Begins
The territorial motto of the island of Guam refers to its proximity to the international date line.

Tarague Beach, on the northern part of Guam, is one example of the beauty of the island.

This aerial view of southern Guam shows the geographic layout of the island.

Territorial Tree

The ifit, or intsiabijuga, is the territorial tree of Guam.

Territorial Bird

The toto, or fruit dove, is the territorial bird of Guam.

Territorial Song

The territorial song of Guam is "Stand Ye Guamanians."

Population

The population of Guam in 1992 was estimated to be 133,152. There are 631.6 people per square mile.

Industries

The principal industries of the island are construction, petroleum refining, tourism, banking, and defense. The chief manufactured products are textiles, petroleum products, and foods.

Agriculture

The chief crops of the island are cabbages, eggplants, cucumbers, long beans, tomatoes, bananas, coconuts, watermelons, yams,

Territorial Capital

Agana is the territorial capital of Guam. This modern city has been rebuilt following its devastation in World War II.

Territorial Seal

The great seal of Guam depicts a coconut palm on the shore and a sailboat nearby on the water. The name "Guam" appears in red across the center of the seal.

Territorial Name

The name Guam comes from the word *guajan*, which means "we have" in the local dialect.

Territorial Flower

The puti tai nobio, or bougainvillea, is the territorial flower of Guam. This woody, tropical vine was named after Louis Antoine de Bougainville, a French explorer and scientist.

cantaloupes, papayas, maize, and sweet potatoes. Livestock is also important in Guam; there are estimated to be 2,000 cattle and 14,000 hogs and pigs on its farms.

Government

Guam is a self-governing, organized, unincorporated territory of the United States, under the supervision of the Department of the Interior. The people of Guam elect a governor and lieutenant governor to four-year terms. The legislature consists of a unicameral, 21-member body elected every two years. The Organic Act of 1950 serves as the territory's constitution. Guamanians also elect a delegate to the U.S. House of Representatives. This delegate, who serves a two-year term, may vote in committee but not on the floor of the House. Guamanians are citizens of the United States but do not vote in national elections.

Sports

Water sports, including swimming, surfing, sailing, fishing, and scuba diving, are popular on Guam. Hunting for deer and boar is among the available activities, as are tennis, golf, and hiking. Cockfighting is an approved sport.

Major Cities

Agana (population 1,139). The capital city of Guam, Agana is located on the west coast of the island at the mouth of the Agana River. Bombs destroyed much of the city during World War II, but it has since been rebuilt. Agana has served as the seat of Guam's government under three flags—those of Spain, Japan, and the United States.

Things to see in Agana: Plaza de España, Kiosko, Azotea, Chocolate House, Tool Shed, Siesta Shed, Spanish Walls, Guam Museum, Dulce Nombre de María Cathedral (1669), and Santo Papa As Juan Pablo Dos Monument.

Places to Visit

The National Park Service maintains one area on Guam: War In The Pacific National Historical Park.

Apugan: Fort Santa Agueda. The fort, which dates from 1800, was constructed of burned limestones mixed with coral rocks.

Inarajan Village: Lanchon Antigo. This replica of a pre-20th century Chamorro village includes exhibits of local artifacts.

Kasamata Hill: Latte Park. Built around 500 A.D., these latte stoves—or house pillars—were moved to this location from Me'pu, an ancient Chamorro settlement.

Merizo: Merizo Conbento. Built in 1856, this is the island's oldest private residence still in use. The Merizo Water Festival is held every August at the Merizo Pier Park.

Tumon Bay: Padre San Vitores Shrine. The shrine is located at the site where Padre San Vitores, a Jesuit missionary, was killed.

Umatac: Fort Nuestra Señora de la Soledad. Built in the early 19th century, this fort overlooks Umatac Bay.

Yigo: South Pacific Memorial Park. Dominated by a tower symbolizing a praying figure, this park, which was dedicated in 1970, is a monument to the U.S. and Japanese determination for peace.

Hikers pause to admire the view from the lower slopes of Mount Lamlam over Cetti Bay on the western side of Guam.

The Land and the Climate

Guam is the largest and southernmost of the Mariana Islands of the West Pacific. The islands of this region are referred to collectively as Micronesia. Guam is some 1,500 miles west of the Philippine Islands and 3,700 miles west of Hawaii.

Guam's 78-mile coastline is fringed with coral reefs. The northern half of the island is a coralline limestone plateau that was originally covered by thick forests. Many of these forests have been cleared for farms and airfields. The southern half of Guam has low mountains of volcanic origin, the steepest of which is Mount Lamlam, 1,334 feet above sea level.

The island has warm weather year-round, with temperatures ranging from 72 to 88 degrees Fahrenheit. Strong seasonal winds called typhoons sometimes hit Guam with destructive force, and rainfall averages 90 inches per year. The island is also subject to occasional earthquakes.

Ferdinand Magellan, the Portuguese explorer commanded the first expedition to sail around the world. After finding the difficult passage, now known as the Strait of Magellan, around Cape Horn, he became the first European known to have crossed the Pacific, discovering many of the small islands of Polynesia. Although Magellan was killed by natives in the Philippines, one of his ships, commanded by Juan Sebastian del Cano, returned to Portugal three years after the expedition began.

The History

It is believed that the native people of Guam, the Chamorro, had originally migrated from the Southeast Asian mainland to Guam. The Portuguese explorer Ferdinand Magellan, serving the court of Spain, discovered Guam and the islands around it in 1521. He called them *Islas de los Ladrones* (the Islands of Thieves), because the people there helped themselves to goods from his ship after supplying him with food and water. The islands were colonized by Spanish missionaries in 1668, and renamed the Marianas in honor of Maria Anna, the queen of Spain. In 1899, after losing the Spanish-American War, Spain ceded Guam to the United States and sold the rest of the

Residents of Guam, an ethnic mix of Pacific peoples, including Indonesians, Filipinos, Koreans, Japanese and Micronesians, enjoy a feast of native dishes – baked bananas, breadfruit and taro, combined with specialties brought to the islands from the rest of the Pacific.

Marianas to Germany. In 1919 Japan obtained a League of Nations mandate over the German Marianas.

Japan attacked Guam on December 7, 1941—the same day it launched the surprise attack on Pearl Harbor, Hawaii, that brought the United States into World War II. The island was captured five days later and was not recovered by U.S. troops until July 21, 1944. The U.S. Navy established its Pacific headquarters there the following year.

Since World War II, Guam has undergone extensive rebuilding and economic rehabilitation. On August 1, 1950, Guam was declared a

territory by the United States, and supervision of the island
was transferred from the navy to the Department of the Interior.
Its people became United States citizens and elected a local
one-house legislature. Beginning in 1970 Guamanians elected their
own governor, who had formerly been appointed by the president
of the United States. After the Communist victory in South Vietnam
in April 1975, more than 100,000 Vietnamese refugees were
temporarily housed in Guam.

Education

The island has 27 public elementary schools and 9 high schools. The
University of Guam located in Mangilao was founded in 1952 and
currently has an enrollment of 2,675.

The People

Only about 25 percent of the people of Guam live in cities like
Agana and Tamuning. Many of them are native Guamanians, called
chamorros—people of Indonesian descent, with a mixture of Filipino
and Spanish blood. They speak both English—the official
language—and the native Chamorro. Other residents are descended
from American, Italian, French, British, Japanese, Chinese, Filipino,
and Mexican settlers. About 52 percent of the population were born
elsewhere. Approximately 48 percent of this population are from Asia,
and about 40 percent of the total population includes U.S. military
personnel and their dependents. Some 95 percent of native Guamanians are Roman Catholic.

Two Lovers Point in Tumon Bay is a spot named for a young Chamorro couple whose love for each other was forbidden. According to legend, they tied their hair together and leapt to their death here.

American Samoa

"April 17, 1900," the date of the first raising of the American flag over the territory, is printed on the top of the Territorial Seal of American Samoa. The *fue*, or fly switch, represents wisdom, while the to'oto'o, or staff, represents authority. The kava bowl symbolizes service to the chief, and the tapa cloth background represents the artistry of the Samoan people.

AMERICAN SAMOA

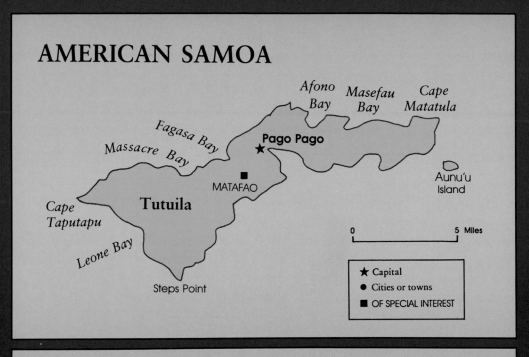

AMERICAN SAMOA

Afono
Bay

Masefau
Bay

Cape
Matatula

Fagasa Bay

Pago Pago
★

Massacre Bay

■
MATAFAO

Aunu'u
Island

Cape
Taputapu

Tutuila

Leone Bay

Steps Point

0   5 Miles

★ Capital
● Cities or towns
■ OF SPECIAL INTEREST

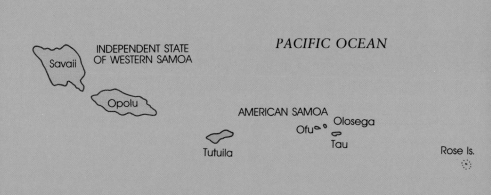

PACIFIC OCEAN

INDEPENDENT STATE
OF WESTERN SAMOA

Savaii

Opolu

AMERICAN SAMOA

Ofu   Olosega

Tutuila

Tau

Rose Is.

AMERICAN SAMOA
At a Glance

Flag

Major Industries: Agriculture, handicrafts

Major Crops: Breadfruit, yams, coconuts, pineapples, bananas

Flower: Paogo (Ula-Fala)

Plant: Ava

Motto: *Samoa Muamua Le Atua* (In Samoa, God Is First)

Song: "Amerika Samoa"

Capital: Pago Pago, Island of Tutuila

Size: 84 square miles
Population: 50,923

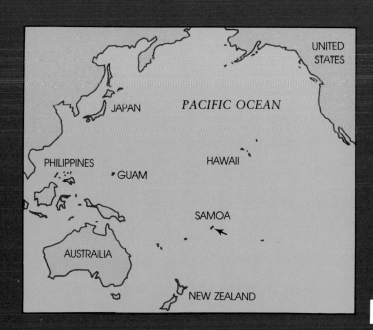

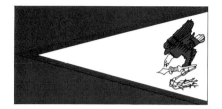

Territorial Flag

The territorial flag of American Samoa, adopted in 1960, consists of a blue field with a white triangle bordered in red pointing to the left. A white-headed eagle, which appears in the triangle, holds a yellow *uatogi*, or war club, representing the power of the state, and a *fue*, or fly switch, signifying wisdom.

Territorial Motto
Samoa Muamua le Atua

The territorial motto of American Samoa means, "In Samoa, God is first."

A breathtaking view of Fagaitus Village.

Baskets, carved wood objects, necklaces, and placemats are just a sampling of the handicrafts made and sold in Samoa.

Territorial Capital

Pago Pago, on the island of Tutuila, is the territorial capital of American Samoa. The Government House is located in Fagatogo, the downtown area of the city.

Territorial Name

American Samoa was named after an ancient Pacific deity.

Territorial Flower

The territorial flower of American Samoa is the paogo, or ula-fala.

Territorial Plant

The ava is the territorial plant of American Samoa.

Territorial Song

The territorial song of American Samoa is "Amerika Samoa."

Population

The population of American Samoa in 1992 was estimated to be 50,923. There are 606.23 persons per square mile. 17.5 percent of the population live in towns and cities.

Industries

The principal industries of the islands are tuna canning and tourism. The chief products are copra (dried coconut), handicrafts, and fish products.

Agriculture

The chief crops of the islands are taro, breadfruit, yams, coconuts, pineapples, oranges, and bananas. The only significant livestock is pigs. There are no important mineral resources.

Government

American Samoa is an unorganized, unincorporated territory of the United States, under the supervision of the Department of the Interior. The people elect a governor and lieutenant governor to four-year terms. Other department heads are appointed by the governor and lieutenant governor and approved by the legislature. The legislature consists of an 18-member senate and a 20-member house of representatives. In addition, one nonvoting delegate from Swain's Island is elected by the adult permanent residents. Senators, who are chosen by *Matai*, the heads of each extended family, serve four-year terms. Representatives, who are chosen by popular vote, serve two-year terms. The most recent constitution was adopted in 1967. American Samoans elect a delegate to the U.S. House of Representatives who may vote in committee, but not on the floor of the House. American Samoans are nationals, but not citizens, of the United States. They do not vote in national elections.

Sports

Water sports such as swimming, diving, sailing, and fishing are extremely popular in American Samoa. The unofficial sport of the islands is *kirikiti*, which is a Polynesian version of cricket played with a hard rubber ball and a three-sided bat.

Major Cities

Pago Pago (population 3,400). Located on the island of Tutuila, Pago Pago is the capital city of American Samoa. The business and administrative center is located at Fagatogo on the west side of the harbor. Pago Pago Bay is the most spectacular deep-water port in the Pacific. It was the site of a U.S. Naval station from 1900 to 1951 and later became a port of call for cruise ships and yachts. There is a strong American influence which can be seen by the presence of the U.S. Navy, and the American goods for sale in the local supermarkets. Pago Pago underwent extensive modernization in the 1960s and was partially successful. Modern public services were developed and its economy was boosted by attracting investments in tuna-fish canning and tourism.

Things to see in Pago Pago: Lyndon B. Johnson Tropical Medicine Center, Government House, and the Aerial Tramway at Mt. Alava.

Places to Visit

Aasu: Massacre Bay. The site of the massacre of Captain Jean François La Pérouse—a French scientist—and his eleven-member expedition in 1787 is marked by a monument erected by France in 1883.

Matafao: Samoan mountains. These lustrous violet-tinged mountains rise to their highest point at 2,141 feet above sea level.

Pago Pago: Dry Goods Store. This store was formerly a hotel where the British author Somerset Maugham wrote his classic short story "Miss Thompson," set in the South Pacific. It was successfully dramatized by John Colton and Clemence Randolph as *Rain*.

Pago Pago Harbor. This scenic deep-water harbor is the only usable seaport in American Samoa.

Events

Arts and Crafts: The Samoan Village (Pago Pago).

On the largest island of Tutuila, a group of Samoans, who share the charm, gaiety and dignity of all Polynesians, enjoy a cricket match.

The Land and the Climate

American Samoa is an unincorporated territory consisting of six small South Pacific islands of the Samoan group, some 4,800 miles southwest of San Francisco. They include Tutuila, Aunu'u, Ta'u, Olosega, Ofu, and Rose. Swain's Island, 210 miles to the northwest, is also administered by the U.S. as part of American Samoa.

Tutuila and Aunu'u have an area of 53 square miles. Ta'u covers 17 square miles, and the islets of Ofu and Olosega, 5 square miles. Swain's Island is about 2 miles square.

Some 70 percent of American Samoa is bush, growing on the slopes of volcanic mountains. Coral reefs surround most of the islands, which have a delightful South Seas climate. The principal export is copra (dried coconut), followed by fish products and handicrafts. Tropical fruits, taro, yams, and citrus crops are cultivated. The only wild animals in Samoa are rats, snakes, and birds. The islands are subject to strong hurricanes and gales between January and March.

The History

American Samoa became U.S. territory by a treaty with Great Britain and Germany in 1899. Local Polynesian chiefs ceded their claims to the islands in 1900 and 1904. Prior to this, the U.S. Navy had used the harbor at Pago Pago as a fueling station, and American Samoa's first administrators were naval officers who ran the islands as a military installation. The welfare of the Samoan people was neglected, except by a handful of missionaries.

In 1951 U.S. president Harry S. Truman transferred responsibility for American Samoa to the Department of the Interior. Since then, the development of the islands has progressed rapidly. Schools have been built, roads paved, housing expanded, and a new jet airport constructed. Because of the islands' spectacular scenery and congenial climate, tourism is a growing industry. In 1978 the first popularly elected Samoan governor and lieutenant governor were inaugurated. Previously, the Secretary of the Interior had appointed the governor. American Samoa has a two-house legislature and an elected delegate to Congress in Washington, D.C.

The People

Most American Samoans are of Polynesian origin, and the largest percentage are Christians. Missionaries converted the majority of Samoans to Christianity, but they retain many of the beliefs and rites of their former animistic religion. Both English and Samoan are spoken. The Samoan language is the oldest Polynesian tongue in use today and it was unwritten until missionaries set it down.

Samoan society is organized around the extended family. The *Matai* is the head of the extended family and is responsible for its welfare. Population is concentrated on the larger islands of Tutuila, Aunu'u, and Ta'u. A few thousand people live on the islets of Ofu and Olosega, and tiny Swain's Island has only about 100 inhabitants.

American influence is obvious in the menu offered to a customer on Tutuila. The native food includes breadfruit, fresh fish and pork, as well as coconut, which may be also used as a flavoring.

Pago Pago Harbor was used as a coaling station for U.S. ships in the early 1900s and continues to service the U.S. Navy.

A young Samoan boy makes a colorful tapa print, one of the most popular crafts in Samoa.

Famous People

Several famous people were born in American Samoa. Here are two:

Tony Solaita 1947-90, Nuuyli. Baseball player

Jack Thompson b. 1956, Tutuila. Football quarterback

Colleges and Universities

There is one college in American Samoa. Listed is its location, date of founding, and enrollment.

American Samoa Community College, Pago Pago, 1970, 1,108

Where To Get More Information

Office of Tourism American Samoan Government Box 1147 Pago Pago, American Samoa 96799 (684) 699-9280

Wake, Midway, and Other Islands

Surrounded by a coral reef, the Midway Islands gave their name to the famous World War II battle. The U.S. victory at Midway prevented the Japanese from gaining a foothold from which they could launch further attacks against Hawaii.

Population

The population of Wake Island, together with its sister islands, Wilkes and Peale, consists of an estimated 300 United States Air Force personnel; the Midway Islands, Sand and Eastern, consist of an estimated 500 U.S. military personnel; Johnston Atoll consists of an estimated 1,000 U.S. government personnel and contractors; Kingman Reef, Palmyra Atoll (which is privately owned), and Howland, Jarvis, and Baker islands have been uninhabited since World War II.

Government

Each of the outlying territories in the Pacific has a civil government under the direct control of, or closely associated with, some federal agency in Washington, D.C. Wake Island is an unincorporated territory of the United States and is administered by the U.S. Air Force; the Midway Islands are an unincorporated territory of the U.S. administered by the Department of the Navy; Johnston Atoll is an unincorporated territory of the U.S. operated by the Defense Nuclear Agency; Howland, Jarvis, and Baker islands are administered by the Department of the Interior; Palmyra Atoll is privately owned, and is administered by the Department of the Interior; and Kingman Reef is under Navy control. The Department of State is responsible for all affairs concerning islands in dispute.

WAKE, MIDWAY, AND OTHER ISLANDS

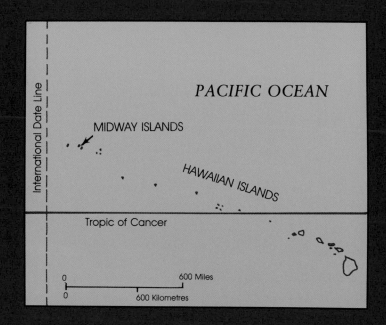

WAKE, MIDWAY, AND OTHER ISLANDS

At a Glance

Size: Wake, Wilkes, and Peale Islands—3 square miles
Midway Islands—2 square miles
Johnston Atoll—1 square mile
Palmyra—4 square miles

Population: Wake, Wilkes, and Peale Islands: 200
Midway Islands: 450

The Land

Wake Island, and its sister islands, Wilkes and Peale, form an atoll (low coral reef) in the west-central Pacific Ocean on the direct route from Hawaii to Hong Kong, some 2,300 miles west of Hawaii. There is no fresh water on these small coral islands, and the scant vegetation consists mainly of shrubs and bushes.

The Midway Islands, Sand and Eastern, are located in the North Pacific, about 1,500 miles northwest of Hawaii. They, too, are coral islands.

Other Pacific islands under U.S. jurisdiction include Johnston Atoll (southwest of Hawaii), Kingman Reef (south of Hawaii), Palmyra (south of Hawaii), and the uninhabited Howland, Jarvis, and Baker Islands (southwest of Hawaii).

The History and People

Wake, Wilkes, and Peale Islands provide a stopping place for ships and airplanes crossing the Pacific. Wake was probably sighted by the Spanish when they explored the Pacific in the 1500s. The first people to land there were the men of the British schooner *Prince William Henry* in 1796.

Wake was explored and surveyed in 1841 by Commander Charles Wilkes of the United States Exploring Expedition, whose naturalist, Titian Peale, investigated the plants and animals there. The group found no indication that the atoll had ever been inhabited.

The United States claimed Wake in 1898 for use on the cable route between San Francisco and Manila. In 1935 it became a base for air traffic crossing the Pacific. When the United States entered World

War II in 1941, Wake became a national defense area. A force of 400 U.S. Marines and about 1,000 civilians held off a Japanese invasion for two weeks, but the islands were finally captured. The Japanese remained there until the war ended in 1945. Since 1972 Wake has been administered by the U.S. Air Force. The U.S. National Weather Service and the U.S. National Oceanographic and Atmospheric Administration have research and monitoring units on the atoll.

The two Midway Islands, Sand and Eastern, were discovered by the United States in 1859 and annexed in 1867. A cable relay station was built there in 1903, and an airport in 1935. One of the most important naval battles in the Pacific theater of operations during World War II was the Battle of Midway, which lasted from June 4 to June 6, 1942. This was the first decisive U.S. victory against the Japanese, and it prevented their occupation of Midway as a base from which they could have attacked Hawaii and other Pacific miliary installations. The Midways are administered by the U.S. Navy Department. No longer a commercial air stop, Midway is a wildlife preserve.

Johnston Atoll is administered by the Nuclear Defense Agency of the Nuclear Regulatory Commission, and Kingman Reef is under U.S. Navy control. Although there are no residents on Howland, Jarvis, and Baker Islands, the Department of the Interior has jurisdiction over them and over the island of Palmyra, which is privately owned.

MICRONESIA

MICRONESIA

At a Glance

Flag

Size: 716 square miles
Population: 191,200

Territorial Flag

The territorial flag of
Micronesia consists of four,
white, five-pointed stars
centered on a dark blue field.

Territorial Capitals

Saipan is the capital of the
Commonwealth of the
Northern Mariana Islands.

The capital of the Federated
States of Micronesia is Palikir,
on the island of Pohnpei. The
United States has appropriated
$15 million toward relocating
the capital about 6 miles to the
southwest, in the Palikir valley.

Majuro is the capital of the
Republic of the Marshall
Islands.

The capital of the Republic of
Palau is Koror.

Territorial Name

The term *Micronesia,* meaning
"little islands," is often used to
refer to an area in the Pacific
Ocean containing more than
2,100 islands. The three major
archipelagoes—the Carolines,
the Marshalls, and the
Marianas—are separated into
four political divisions. These
are the Commonwealth of the
Northern Mariana Islands, the
Federated States of Micronesia,
the Republic of the Marshall
Islands, and the Republic of
Palau.

Population

The population of the
Commonwealth of the
Northern Mariana Islands in
1990 was estimated to be
23,300. There are 126.6
persons per square mile—16.0
percent of the population live
in towns and cities. Only six
of the islands are inhabited.

The population of the
Federated States of Micronesia
in 1990 was estimated to be
108,000. There are 398.5
persons per square mile—19.4
percent of the population live
in towns and cities.

The population of the
Republic of the Marshall
Islands in 1990 was estimated
to be 45,600. There are 651.4
persons per square mile—47.8
percent of the population live
in towns and cities.

The population of the
Republic of Palau in 1990 was
estimated to be 14,300. There
are 80.8 persons per square
mile—51.4 percent of the
population live in towns and
cities. Only eight of the
islands are permanently
inhabited.

Industries

The principal industries of
Micronesia are tourism and
construction. The chief
manufactured products are
craft items made from shells,
wood, and pearls.

Agriculture

The chief crops of Micronesia
are coffee, coconuts, fruits, and
tobacco from the
Commonwealth of the
Northern Mariana Islands;
copra, black pepper, tropical
fruits and vegetables,
coconuts, cassavas, and sweet
potatoes from the Federated

States of Micronesia; coconuts, cacao, taro, breadfruit, fruits, and copra from the Republic of the Marshall Islands; and coconut, copra, cassavas, and sweet potatoes from the Republic of Palau. Most crops grown on the islands are for local consumption. The chief **exported crop is copra, although vegetables are also exported** from the Northern Marianas. Livestock is also important in Micronesia. Cattle and pigs are raised in the Northern Mariana Islands; pigs, cattle, and goats in the Marshall Islands; and pigs and chickens in the Federated States of Micronesia. Deep seabed minerals, marine products, and forests are important natural resources. In addition, there are phosphate deposits in the Marshall Islands and gold in Palau. Commercial fishing is a minor economic activity in Palau and the Marshall Islands.

Government

From 1947 to 1986, Micronesia was known as the United States Trust Territory of the Pacific Islands. In 1986, the trusteeship was dissolved and the Federated States of Micronesia, the Republic of the Marshall Islands, and the Republic of Palau signed a Compact of Free Association with the United States. At the same time, the Northern Mariana Islands became a commonwealth of the U.S. Because Palauans did not approve the Compact, their republic is still administered by the trusteeship.

Each of the four political divisions of Micronesia is self-governing. The people of the Commonwealth of the Northern Mariana Islands elect a governor and lieutenant governor. The legislature consists of a nine-member senate and a 15-member house of representatives. Senators serve four-year terms and representatives serve two-year terms. The most recent constitution was adopted in 1978. The people of the Northern Marianas are citizens of the United States, but do not vote in national elections.

The president and vice-president of the Federated States of Micronesia are elected from among the members of the National Congress of the Federated States of Micronesia, which is the legislative body of the territory. The legislature is unicameral, and its senators are elected by the people. The most recent constitution was adopted in 1979. Each of the four states of the territory— Ponape, Yap, Truk, and Kosrae—elects its own legislature and governor.

The president of the Republic of the Marshall Islands is elected by a 33-member, unicameral parliament, or *Nitijela*. He appoints a Cabinet of Ministers. A Council of *Iroij*, or chiefs, serves as a consultative body on matters involving traditional law and custom. The most recent constitution was adopted in 1979.

The president and vice-president of the Republic of Palau are elected by the people. A Council of Chiefs advises the president on matters of traditional law and customs. The legislature of Palau consists of a house of delegates and a senate. The most recent constitution went into effect in 1980.

Major Cities
Palikir, Federated States of Micronesia (population 5,549). Palikir is the capital and largest city of the Federated States of Micronesia.

Koror, Republic of Palau (population 10,501). Koror is the capital and largest city of the Republic of Palau.

Majuro, Marshall Islands (population 14,267). The capital and largest city of the Marshall Islands, Majuro is a large atoll, with many of its islands connected by roads. The city is the administrative center of the islands and offers excellent swimming at many of its beaches.

Yap stone was the traditional currency of the island. As the huge stones were too large to move, the title, or ownership, of the stones would be exchanged for goods or services.

Saipan, Northern Mariana Islands (population 38,896). The capital and largest city of the Northern Mariana Islands, Saipan is a busy commercial center. The remains of several American airfields built during World War II may still be seen.

Things to see in Saipan: Suicide Cliff, the old Japanese jail, the last Japanese command post, the old Japanese hospital, Peace Memorial, Sugar King monument, blue grotto, and Bird Island.

Colleges and Universities
The College of Micronesia is the only institute of higher education in Micronesia. The three campuses of the college are the School of Nursing on Saipan, Community College of Micronesia on Ponape, and the Micronesian Occupational College on Palau.

A monument honors those Korean troops, fighting with the Japanese, who died defending Saipan in June, 1944.

The Land

Bird Island lies off the northern coast of Saipan, the main island in the Mariana chain.

Micronesia is the common name for what is officially the United States Trust Territory of the Pacific Islands. It includes three major archipelagoes, or groups of small islands, scattered over 3 million square miles of the Pacific. These systems are the Caroline, Marshall, and Mariana Islands. (Although Guam is part of the Marianas, it is not included in the Trust Territory, since it has its own legislature and governor.)

The Caroline Islands are just north of the equator, between the Marshall Islands and the Philippines. There are more than 930 islands in this archipelago, many of them volcanic, with luxuriant vegetation; others are barren coral islands. Fish products, copra (dried coconut) handicrafts, and vegetables are exported from the larger islands, the best known of which are the World War II Japanese strongholds of Belau, Peleliu, Truk, and Yap.

For many years, the United States carried out hydrogen and atomic bomb testing near the atolls of Bikini and Enewetak. The native Micronesians were removed to other islands, but recently 55 natives pressured the U. S. government to return home.

The Marshall Islands are some 2,200 miles southwest of Hawaii. The 34 small islands in this archipelago are primarily coral. The people of the Marshalls cultivate palm and breadfruit trees, and their livelihood depends mainly on copra and fish. The climate is tropical, but ocean breezes cool the air. Rainfall is light in the northern islands, and heavy further south. The best known of the Marshall Islands are Bikini and Enewetak Atolls, where the United States conducted nuclear tests after World War II, and Kwajalein, the site of a wartime battle.

The 15 Mariana Islands are volcanic in origin, part of a submerged mountain chain that extends 1,565 miles from Guam almost to Japan. The 10 northern Marianas are primarily rugged, some of them with active volcanoes that erupt from time to time. The five southerly islands, which are older than the others, have no active volcanoes. Manganese and phosphate are mined in the Marianas, and farmers produce copra and food crops. The group's most important islands, apart from Guam, are Pagan, Agrihan, Anatahan, Rota, Saipan, and Tinian.

The History

In 1527 Spain claimed the Carolines, which it sold to Germany in 1899, after the Spanish-American War. During World War I, Japan took control of all Micronesia, including the Carolines, and the League of Nations awarded the Japanese a mandate over the islands after the war. During World War II, U.S. forces captured some of the islands, including Peleliu, after heavy fighting. Japan surrendered in 1945, and the United Nations made the United States trustee of the Carolines as part of the Trust Territory of the Pacific Islands.

The first European to visit what became known as the Marshall Islands was probably a Spanish navigator, Alvaro de Saavedra, who

A young Saipanese girl husks coconuts to sell them to Japanese tourists. Many Japanese visit Saipan for the tropical beaches and pleasant climate.

sailed the central Pacific in 1529. In 1788 John Marshall, an English sea captain, explored the islands that were named for him. In 1866 Germany gained control of the Marshalls, which it bought from Spain in 1899. After World War I, they passed to Japanese control through the League of Nations mandate. In 1933 Japan left the League of Nations, sealed off the Marshalls to Europeans, and built military bases on some of the islands as part of the expansionist policy that brought the Japanese Empire into World War II. The United States captured Enewetak and Kwajalein in 1944 and ultimately took control of all the Marshall Islands.

Ferdinand Magellan, a Portuguese navigator in the service of Spain, discovered what are now the Marianas in 1521. Spanish missionaries arrived in 1668, and Spain governed the islands until the Spanish-American War of 1898, after which it sold all the Marianas except Guam to Germany. The Japanese took control of the islands during World War I and held them until 1944, when U.S. forces defeated them in the World War II battles for Guam, Saipan, and Tinian. In 1947 all the Mariana Islands except Guam became part of the U.S. Trust Territory of the Pacific Islands. The Northern Marianas, as they are called, are currently seeking U.S. commonwealth status.

The People

The people of the Trust Territory are primarily Micronesians, whose ancestry includes Melanesian, Polynesian, and Malaysian stock. Only 98 of the Territory's 2,141 islands are inhabited.

Further Reading

General

Grabowski, John F. and Patricia A. Grabowski. *State Reports: U.S. Territories and Possessions*. New York: Chelsea House, 1992.

Howe, K.R. *Where the Waves Fall: A New South Sea Island History from First Settlement to Colonial Rule*. 1984.

Puerto Rico

Colorado, Antonio J. *The First Book of Puerto Rico*, 2nd ed. New York: Franklin Watts, 1972.

Kent, Deborah. *America the Beautiful: Puerto Rico*. Chicago: Childrens Press, 1991.

McKown, Robin. *The Image of Puerto Rico: Its History and Its People, One the Island— One the Mainland*. New York: McGraw-Hill, 1973.

Perl, Lila. *Puerto Rico: Island Between Two Worlds*. New York: William Morrow, 1979.

Singer, Julia. *We All Come from Someplace: Children of Puerto Rico*. New York: Atheneum, 1976.

Steiner, Stanley. *The Islands: The Worlds of the Puerto Ricans*. New York: Harper & Row, 1974.

United States Virgin Islands

Creque, Darwin D. *The U.S. Virgins and the Eastern Caribbean*. Whitmore, 1968.

Eggleston, George T., *Virgin Islands*. Melbourne, FL: Krieger, 1973.

Moore, James E. *Everybody's Virgin Islands*. New York: Lippincott, 1979.

Guam

Carano, Paul, and Pedro C. Sanchez. *A Complete History of Guam*. Rutland, VT: Tuttle, 1964.

Farrell, Don A. *Guam: 1898- 1918*. Micronesian, 1985.

Ishikawa, Wes. *The Elder Guamanians*. Campile, 1977.

Lutz, William. *Guam*. 1987.

American Samoa

Henry, Fred. *Samoa, an Early History*. 1980.

Micronesia

Alkire, William H. *An Introduction to the Peoples and Cultures of Micronesia*, 2nd ed. 1977.

Brower, Kenneth. *Micronesia: The Land, the People and the Sea*. Baton Rouge: Louisiana State University Press, 1982.

Hughes, Daniel T., and Sherwood G. Lingenfelter. *Political Development in Micronesia*. Columbus: Ohio State University Press, 1974.

Nevin, David. *The American Touch in Micronesia*. New York: Norton, 1977.

Numbers in italics refer to illustrations

Picture Credits

American Samoa Government Office of Tourism: pp. 71, 74-75, 76, 80; Culver: pp. 54, 67; Courtesy of Embassy of the Federated States of Micronesia (Dick Merritt): p. 88; John Florian: pp. 6-7, 19, 20-21, 22, 30, 32, 33, 34; Courtesy of Guam Visitors Bureau: pp. 59, 62-63, 64, 70; Dave Kleinman: pp. 30-31; Library of Congress: p. 26; New York Public Library: pp. 28, 49; Courtesy of Puerto Rico Travel Commission: pp. 5, 8-9, 10, 12, 13, 14, 15, 16, 17; The Rowland Company: pp. 4 (top), 18, 23, 24-25, 27, 29, 35, 36; Courtesy of U.S. Virgin Islands Division of Tourism: pp. 39, 42-43, 44, 45, 46, 47, 48, 55; Wide World: pp. 37, 78, 79, 81, 90-91.
Cover photos courtesy of American Samoa Government Office of Tourism; the Rowland Company; and U.S. Virgin Islands Division of Tourism.